Artificial Intelligence in Water Quality Marketing:
A Practical Guide to AI-Powered Lead Generation

DALE "DATADALE" FILHABER

CONTENTS

Introduction: Embracing AI in Marketing 4
The Evolution of Artificial Intelligence 5
Exploring the Various Types of AI 6
Your New Assistant: AI in Marketing 9
Crafting Direct Mail Letters with AI 10
Designing Impactful Postcards Using AI 13
Blogging Made Easy with AI 17
Elevating Social Media Engagement through AI 26
A Note About Hashtags 28
Streamlining Email Campaigns with AI 29
Boosting Open Rates: AI-Enhanced Email Subject Lines 32
The Art of AI-Generated Imagery 33
Navigating AI and Copyright Laws 38
Conclusion: The Future of AI in Marketing 39
About the Author: Dale "Data Dale" Filhaber 40
Dataman Group Direct 41

INTRODUCTION: EMBRACING AI IN MARKETING

I've been working with Water Quality Dealers for a long time. In that time, I've seen a tremendous improvement in the professionalism of marketing materials put out by the industry.

At the last two WQA conferences, I presented information on AI – Artificial Intelligence – and how it can be a real driver in your marketing efforts. I've spoken with many Dealers about how they can use AI to develop their creative and enhance their lead generation.

Yes, I know I don't sell AI. But when you have better marketing material, it improves the response you'll get from the marketing lists we provide. You want more leads, right?

A very smart friend of mine, Sue Gleason from Charger Water, said "AI won't replace Marketers, but Marketers who use AI will replace Marketers who don't."

This book will help you start your journey and give you some real insight into how Artificial Intelligence – AI – can help you with some of your marketing responsibilities. Once you get the gist of how to use AI and when to use AI, you will save time with your copy and branding. This will ultimately save you dollars and help you craft a stand-out brand identity of your own.

It's all about generating leads for your dealership. That's what translates into dollars.

This book has a lot of great examples of creatives and offers that works in the water quality market. Learn from them and personalize for your own Dealership.

THE EVOLUTION OF ARTIFICIAL INTELLIGENCE

Artificial Intelligence (AI) traces its roots back to the mid-20th century, sparked by the pioneering work of Alan Turing and others who asked whether machines could think. Turing's 1950 paper, "Computing Machinery and Intelligence," introduced the concept of a machine that could simulate human reasoning.

BTW - Do any of you remember the movie The Imitation Game with Benedict Cumberbatch when he portrayed Alan Turing inventing the Enigma?

The official birth of AI as a distinct field occurred at a 1956 workshop at Dartmouth College, where the term "Artificial Intelligence" was coined by John McCarthy. Early optimism was high, and researchers initially predicted that a fully intelligent machine would be developed within a generation.

Progress through the 1960s and 70s was marked by the development of algorithms and early neural networks. However, AI faced periods of reduced funding and interest, known as "AI winters," during the late 70s and late 80s, due to unmet expectations and technical limitations.

A resurgence in the late 1990s and early 2000s came with advances in machine learning and the internet, providing vast amounts of data and improved computational power. The success of IBM's Deep Blue against chess champion Garry Kasparov in 1997 and later developments in natural language processing and robotics reinvigorated the field.

In the 2010s, AI saw breakthroughs with deep learning, significantly enhancing capabilities in voice recognition, image processing, and strategic game playing, exemplified by systems like IBM Watson and Google's AlphaGo.

Today, we use AI on so many of our daily life functions that we don't even realize we're using it. I ask Alexa to turn on the lights. I get in the car and ask Siri for directions. I look at Facebook and see ads directed at me because of past purchases. We don't even think of some of the things we use during the day as AI.

EXPLORING THE VARIOUS TYPES OF AI

We see the term AI in the headlines of lots of news reports, on TV. Everybody is talking about it but many people I speak with don't understand the nuances on the term AI.

There are two types of AI; Predictive and Generative.

PREDICTIVE AI

Predictive AI is all about looking ahead. It uses the data you feed it to forecast what might happen next, whether that's figuring out what comes out of a dataset or categorizing things based on past trends.

You see this type of AI in action when your email app filters out spam, or when banks decide who gets credit. It's also behind the scenes in weather predictions—really, it's in play anytime you need to guess future outcomes based on what's happened before.

This type of AI relies heavily on supervised learning, meaning it learns from examples that are already labeled. The tools of the trade here include regression models, decision trees, support vector machines, and specially designed neural networks that tackle various forecasting tasks.

EXAMPLES OF PREDICTIVE AI

Let's use **Netflix** as an example.

Netflix uses predictive AI to suggest movies and TV shows to its users based on their viewing history. The system analyzes patterns in user behavior, preferences, and similarities in content to predict and recommend media that the viewer is likely to enjoy.

By personalizing the content, Netflix keeps viewers engaged. People like getting suggestions that make sense based on the shows they watched in the past. This helps Netflix maintain its subscriber base.

Another great example is Google Maps Traffic Predictions:

Google Maps employs predictive AI to forecast traffic conditions and estimate travel times. It analyzes historical traffic data, current road conditions, and events that might affect traffic, and predicts traffic build-up and suggests optimal routes in real-time.

Take it a step further, Google Maps can plan routes to a given address and at the same time, help me avoid traffic jams and detours.

Don't you hate it when you look at your route guidance screen and see that solid red "traffic jam" line coming up? But, I love it when my car re-routes me,

This type of AI has become an indispensable tool for daily navigation in urban environments.

GENERATIVE AI

The other classification of AI is Generative AI.

Generative AI is the creative cousin in the AI family. It's not just analyzing data but actually creating new material—like images, tunes, text, or videos—that mirror real-world examples but are fresh and unique.

This is the tech behind all the marketing substance we're talking about it this book. Generative AI the power behind deepfakes, AI-powered art creators, and tools that churn out new content for marketing and entertainment.

AI keeps learning. Sometimes we wonder what is fake and what is real. AI uses variational autoencoders, and specific neural networks built to generate new patterns and ideas, not just make predictions or sort data. These techniques help it dream up completely new creations.

How do you know what is fake and what is real. One cool method they use is GANs (Generative Adversarial Networks), where two AI models—the generator and discriminator—team up to refine and produce top-notch creative outputs.

This technology has been a game-changer in fields requiring realistic image, video, and voice generation, and it's widely used in creative applications such as art generation, video game content creation, and more.

EXAMPLES OF GENERATIVE AI

I used DALL.E which is an AI program, to create a unique image for one of my blogs.

ME to DALL.E:

Create a photo of a child drinking a clear glass of water in a brightly lit kitchen:

AI goes much further than just creating simple images. It is able to actually generate images that are so real we have no idea whether they are real or not. These technologies use neural networks to transform photos into the styles of various famous artists. DeepArt and similar tools apply styles from iconic paintings to user-uploaded photographs, effectively "repainting" the photo in a completely new style.

These tools have popularized AI art, allowing users to create novel and visually captivating images without needing any artistic skills, like I did just above. They have also sparked discussions about creativity and the role of AI in art. The same thing is going on in the Entertainment industry. Lots of conversations about the ownership of material.

Another great example is **ChatGPT by OpenAI:**

ChatGPT is a generative AI model designed to generate human-like text based on the prompt it receives. It uses patterns learned from a vast dataset to produce coherent and contextually relevant responses across various topics.

ChatGPT has been widely used for tasks ranging from writing assistance, tutoring, customer service, to entertainment. Its famous for its ability to interact in a conversational manner - for example I can prompt my ChatGPT in simple English – no special formulas or programs. That's why it's a popular tool for both personal and professional use – and a great example that illustrates the practical applications of generative language models.

Generative AI can create new, useful content that mimics human creativity, ranging from visual arts to written communication.

But always remember, your AI is your marketing assistant. You are the boss.

YOUR NEW ASSISTANT: AI IN MARKETING

Most of the examples I am using in this book are from ChatGPT 4.0. Yes, there are lots of other AI platforms that can help you write copy.

The reason I chose ChatGPT for this book – and to give to examples - is that ChatGPT is readily available and offers a free edition as well as a paid edition. Many existing programs are adding AI features to provide their customers with AI options within their systems. For example, I use Constant Contact to send enewsletters to my customers. Constant Contact now offers an AI feature. They want you to stay within their framework (for a price). Salesforce, Google – everyone has an AI feature.

The most important thing you need to do when you use AI is learn how to prompt the system to give you the material you want.

PROMPTING

The term "prompt" when we're talking about AI actually comes from old-school computer and language use. In the computer world, a "prompt" is what you see when the computer is ready to take your input—like a little cue or nudge. That idea just flowed into AI, where a prompt does the same thing: it nudges the AI to kick into gear and deliver what you're asking for.

From a language point of view, to "prompt" someone means to push them to say or do something. So when you toss a prompt to an AI, you're basically pushing it to spit out the response you need. It's a simple but spot-on term because it's all about getting the AI rolling in the right direction based on your cue.

Be specific. Tell your AI if you're looking for a blog or a post. Communicate how many words you're looking for. Cue the kind of writing style you're looking for.

And just as you learn from AI, it learns from you, too.

One last, very important marketing caveat before we dive in. It doesn't matter how great your letter, postcard or email subject line is - you need to be directing those communications to the right targeted audience.

If you are marketing to new homeowners, your message should reference them; your offer should be tailored to them. If you're marketing to families with children, you want to make sure you are speaking to them.

Make sure you tell your AI the audience you're looking to reach. That way, your output is personalized to your target group.

CRAFTING DIRECT MAIL LETTERS WITH AI

Many of you joined us at the panel session on AI at the last WQA conference. I've gotten a lot of requests for more information about using AI, how to prompt, and the different opportunities there are to use AI in marketing.

I asked my ChatGPT how best to use AI to develop a direct mail letter. Then to create an example of a well-written letter for water filter sales.

Remember, we use AI to help us frame what we want. We are not going to just go with it. We are going to adapt, edit, and enhance whatever AI provides. But let it help guide you. When you use artificial intelligence to craft a compelling direct mail letter, you can significantly enhance your marketing strategies. Even for products like water filters where educating the consumer plays a crucial role. AI can help personalize content, analyze customer data for better targeting, and optimize messaging for increased engagement.

THE 4 STEPS TO CREATING A DIRECT MAIL LETTER – OR ANY KIND OF TARGETED MARKETING

Step 1: Understand Your Audience

Before drafting your letter, you need to have a deep understanding of your audience. AI can analyze customer data to identify patterns, preferences, and needs. For water filter sales, your target audience might include health-conscious individuals, families concerned about water quality, or environmentally aware consumers.

Use AI to segment your audience and tailor your message for that particular segment.

Step 2: Create Compelling Content with AI

AI tools can assist in generating persuasive and personalized content. Start with a clear message about the benefits of using a water filter, such as improved health, better tasting water, or environmental conservation.

Then you can use AI to craft a narrative that resonates with your audience's concerns and desires. For example, if you are targeting families, emphasize the health benefits and the importance of clean water for children's development.

Step 3: Personalize Your Letter

Personalization is key to direct mail success. And I don't just mean using someone's name. If you have a great CRM tool, AI can help customize each letter based on the recipient's previous interactions, purchase history, and preferences.

If we're talking about lead generation, include you'll want to specific concerns or interests they have demonstrated. For example, there may be a segment of your audience who has expressed interested in eco-friendly products. Your letter to them needs to highlight the environmental benefits of your water filters.

Step 4: Optimize and Test Your Letter

Use AI to test different versions of your letter, including variations in headlines, calls to action (CTAs), and layout. That way you can analyze the performance of each version to determine what works best.

This process helps refine your approach and ensures that your final product is as effective as possible.

ME to ChatGPT:

Create a general direct mail letter for water filtration dealers:

ChatGPT

Dear [Name],

Imagine a world where your family's health and well-being are never compromised by the water you drink. With [Your Brand]'s advanced water filtration system, this vision becomes reality. Our state-of-the-art filters remove impurities, ensuring every sip is not just safe, but also deliciously refreshing.

As a [specific attribute, e.g., environmentally conscious] individual, you understand the importance of clean water. Not just for the health benefits, but also for the peace of mind it brings. Our eco-friendly filters are designed with sustainability in mind, helping to reduce plastic bottle waste and conserve our planet's precious resources.

For a limited time, we're offering an exclusive promotion just for you. Try our water filter system risk-free and see the difference for yourself. Plus, as a special thank you, we'll include a complimentary [incentive, e.g., year's supply of filters] with your purchase.

ChatGPT

Don't miss out on this opportunity to enhance your family's quality of life. Act now and join the thousands of satisfied customers who trust [Your Brand] to keep their water pure, healthy, and delicious.

Warmest regards,

Name]

[Your Position]

[Contact Information]

When you create a direct mail letter for water filter sales, or any product, using AI can dramatically improve your marketing efforts. By understanding your audience, creating compelling and personalized content, and continuously optimizing your approach, you can increase engagement and drive sales. Remember, the key to a successful direct mail campaign lies in its relevance and personal touch, something AI can significantly enhance.

In the U.S., most of our dealers use postcards rather than letters. But just think, what if someone got a letter with a good envelope teaser that offers low cost financing......it's just something a recipient might open up.

Everything is worth a test.

DESIGNING IMPACTFUL POSTCARDS USING AI

Many of our water filtration dealers use postcards to generate leads. But, how do you decide what to write. What copy will work best?

I used ChatGPT to help me take a look at the options.

As always, remember that we use AI to help us formulate what we're doing. It's not the end-all, be-all. You need to make sure you modify for your specific Dealership.

I am putting my prompts in blue.

ME to ChatGPT:

Create 4 bullet points for postcard copy for water filtration dealers

ChatGPT

Ensure Pure, Healthy Drinking Water: Equip your home with the latest in water filtration technology. Experience the peace of mind that comes with knowing every drop of water in your home is clean, pure, and free from harmful contaminants.

Taste the Difference: Our advanced water filtration systems not only provide safer water but also improve the taste, odor, and clarity of your water. Enjoy refreshing and delicious water straight from your tap, every time.

Eco-Friendly and Cost-Effective: Say goodbye to the expense and environmental impact of bottled water. Our sustainable water filtration solutions reduce plastic waste and save you money in the long run, all while ensuring endless access to pure water.

Professional Installation and Service: Trust our experienced team for a hassle-free installation process and ongoing support. With regular maintenance and expert advice, your water filtration system will provide superior water quality for years to come.

ME to ChatGPT:

Way too wordy for postcard copy. Please trim

ChatGPT

Pure Water, Pure Peace of Mind: Clean and safe, right from your tap.
Taste the Clarity: Better tasting, odorless water.
Save Money, Save the Planet: Ditch bottled water for good.
Expert Care, Effortless Maintenance: Hassle-free installation and support.

ME to ChatGPT:

That's good. Can you provide a worthy offer

ChatGPT

Limited Time Offer: Get 20% Off Installation!
Unlock cleaner, healthier water today and save on your initial setup. Act now—offer ends soon!

ME to ChatGPT:

OK, why did you choose that?

ChatGPT

I chose a 20% off installation offer because it strikes a balance between appealing to new customers and being financially sensible for the business. Here's why it's effective:

Immediate Value: A discount on installation provides immediate, tangible savings, making the decision to invest in a water filtration system more attractive.

Encourages Quick Decisions: Limited-time offers create a sense of urgency, encouraging potential customers to act quickly to take advantage of the savings.

Focus on Long-Term Benefits: By discounting the installation rather than the system itself, it highlights the quality and value of the product. Customers are getting a high-quality system at full value, with the bonus of cheaper installation.

Attracts Price-Sensitive Customers: It makes the service more accessible to those who may be on the fence due to cost concerns, expanding the customer base.

This type of offer is often used because it works well for both the business and the consumer, balancing initial incentives with long-term value and relationships.

ME to ChatGPT:

Can you create a tag line for a water quality business that underscores competence and value

ChatGPT

"Clear Quality, Pure Value: Expertise in Every Drop"

What you can see is that I had a "conversation" with ChatGPT. The first set of bullet points was way too wordy. So, I asked ChatGPT to redo them. AI does not get insulted. You can ask for multiple changes or tweaks.

Then, I asked ChatGPT to come up with an offer for the postcard. Remember, you always want to make a good offer to entice people to act. The better your offer, the more apt your prospect will be to respond. BTW - with direct mail, you are marketing to a highly targeted audience. Because of this, you can afford to make a better offer than you might in a newspaper ad. Remember, this is all about lead generation.

ChatGPT suggested a 20% off installation offer. When I asked ChatGPT why it came up with that offer, it was very specific about its' reasoning. You might have another offer in mind. Run it by your AI.

Finally, I asked ChatGPT to come up with a tag line. Companies use taglines in marketing campaigns to create a lasting impression on consumers. Taglines tell consumers about your brand's values, unique selling point and personality. It goes beyond individual products and helps you reframe your value proposition.

ChatGPT suggested "Clear Quality, Pure Value: Expertise in Every Drop" (BTW- I Love this)

ME to ChatGPT:

OK, why did you choose that tag line

ChatGPT

I chose "Clear Quality, Pure Value: Expertise in Every Drop" for several reasons, aiming to highlight both competence and value, which are crucial for a water quality business:

Clarity in Communication: The word "Clear" not only refers to the purity and cleanliness of the water but also suggests transparency and honesty in business practices.

Quality and Value Front and Center: By stating "Quality" and "Value" prominently, the tagline assures customers of high-quality products and services that offer great worth for their investment.

Expertise Highlighted: The phrase "Expertise in Every Drop" underscores the company's thorough knowledge and specialization in water quality. It reassures customers that every aspect of their service, from consultation to installation and maintenance, is handled with professional care and know-how.

Emotional Appeal: Water is a vital part of daily life, and the tagline's emphasis on every drop speaks to the meticulous attention to detail the company offers, reinforcing the message that they genuinely care about the health and wellbeing of their customers.

This tagline is designed to resonate with the target audience by assuring them of the company's commitment to delivering superior service and value, backed by expert knowledge and care.

BLOGGING MADE EASY WITH AI

OK, maybe not easy – but definitely easier!

You can't just tell your AI to create a blog. You need to direct AI as to topic, audience and writing style. You also have to be very specific about the length. We call this prompting,

Here's an example of a give and take between me and ChatGPT about writing a blog

ME to ChatGPT:

How many words should be in a blog?

ChatGPT

There is no strict rule for the number of words in a blog post, as it can vary based on several factors including the topic, audience, and writing style. However, many bloggers aim for a word count that is sufficient to thoroughly cover the topic while still maintaining the reader's interest.

Generally, a typical blog post ranges from 500 to 2,000 words, but some may be shorter or longer depending on the content. Shorter posts can be concise and to the point, while longer posts allow for more in-depth exploration of a topic.

Ultimately, the most important factor is to prioritize quality content that engages readers and provides value, regardless of the specific word count.

ME to ChatGPT:

What would be a good topic for a blog about water quality?

ChatGPT

A good topic for a blog about water quality could be "The Impact of Industrial Pollution on Local Water Sources." This topic allows for exploration of how industrial activities such as manufacturing, mining, and chemical processing can contribute to water pollution, affecting local communities and ecosystems. The blog could discuss specific case studies or examples, delve into the environmental and health implications of industrial pollution in water sources, and highlight potential solutions or mitigation efforts. This topic has relevance to both environmental enthusiasts and individuals interested in public health and sustainability, making it potentially engaging for a wide audience.

ME to ChatGPT:

Can you talk about how an in-home water filtration system can protect people from this?

ChatGPT

Certainly!

An in-home water filtration system can play a crucial role in protecting people from the impacts of industrial pollution and other contaminants in their water supply. Here's how:

- **Removal of Chemicals and Heavy Metals**: Many industrial pollutants, such as heavy metals like lead, mercury, and arsenic, can leach into groundwater sources and contaminate drinking water supplies. High-quality water filtration systems, especially those with activated carbon or reverse osmosis technology, are effective at removing these harmful substances from water, making it safe for consumption.
- **Reduction of Microbial Contaminants**: Industrial pollution can also introduce microbial contaminants like bacteria, viruses, and protozoa into water sources, posing significant health risks. Filtration systems equipped with UV sterilization or microbiological filters can effectively eliminate these pathogens, ensuring that the water is microbiologically safe to drink.

ChatGPT

- **Protection Against Chemical Runoff**: Industrial activities often involve the use of chemicals and pesticides, which can seep into groundwater and contaminate water sources near agricultural areas or industrial sites. Water filtration systems can target and remove these chemical contaminants, providing an additional layer of protection against the harmful effects of chemical runoff.
- **Peace of Mind**: Having an in-home water filtration system provides peace of mind to homeowners, knowing that they have control over the quality of their drinking water. This is particularly important in areas where industrial pollution or other environmental concerns may compromise the safety of the municipal water supply.
- **Long-term Cost Savings**: While the initial investment in a water filtration system may seem significant, it can result in long-term cost savings compared to purchasing bottled water or relying on other temporary solutions. Additionally, investing in a filtration system can potentially reduce healthcare costs associated with waterborne illnesses or long-term exposure to contaminants.

Overall, an in-home water filtration system serves as a proactive measure to safeguard against the potential health risks associated with industrial pollution and other water contaminants, ensuring that households have access to clean, safe drinking water.

ME to ChatGPT:

Can you re-write this in a friendlier tone?

ChatGPT

Absolutely! Here's a friendlier version:

"Hey there! Ever wondered how having a water filter at home can really make a difference? Let's dive in!

- **Bye-bye Nasty Stuff**: Picture this – your filter is like a superhero, swooping in to rescue your water from yucky things like lead and other chemicals that sneak into water from factories and industries. With activated carbon or reverse osmosis magic, these filters zap away those baddies, leaving you with clean, safe water to drink.
- **Bye-bye Germs**: Say adios to those pesky microbes too! Some filters have special powers, like UV light or microscopic filters, that zap away bacteria, viruses, and other tiny troublemakers that can make you sick.
- **Saving the Day from Chemicals**: Filters also come to the rescue against chemicals and pesticides that might find their way into your water from farms or factories nearby. They're like your water's own bodyguard, keeping it safe from harmful stuff.
- **Feel-Good Factor**: Having a filter at home gives you peace of mind. You can trust that your water is clean and safe for you and your family, even if there are concerns about pollution in your area.
- **Save Money, Stay Healthy**: Sure, getting a water filter might seem like a splurge at first, but think about it – you'll save money in the long run compared to buying bottled water all the time. Plus, you'll be protecting your health and avoiding potential doctor bills from water-related illnesses.

So, having a water filter isn't just about having clean water – it's like having a superhero buddy, keeping you healthy and happy every time you take a sip!"

ME to ChatGPT:

OK, Not too friendly - still needs to sound professional

ChatGPT

Of course, let's maintain a professional tone while keeping it engaging. Here's a more professionally toned rewrite:

- **Effective Contaminant Removal**: A home water filtration system serves as a reliable barrier against contaminants introduced into water sources by industrial activities. Employing technologies such as activated carbon and reverse osmosis, these systems effectively eliminate harmful substances like heavy metals and chemicals, ensuring the safety of your drinking water.
- **Microbial Protection**: In addition to chemical contaminants, water filters equipped with UV sterilization or microbiological filters offer robust protection against microbial pathogens. These features are essential in safeguarding against waterborne illnesses caused by bacteria, viruses, and protozoa.
- **Mitigating Chemical Runoff**: Filters also play a vital role in mitigating the effects of chemical runoff from agricultural and industrial areas. By targeting and removing chemical pollutants, they contribute to the preservation of water quality and protect against potential health hazards associated with exposure to these substances.
- **Assurance and Peace of Mind**: Investing in a home water filtration system provides homeowners with assurance regarding the quality and safety of their drinking water. This is particularly significant in regions where concerns about industrial pollution or environmental contaminants exist, offering peace of mind to residents.
- **Long-term Financial and Health Benefits**: While the initial investment in a filtration system may seem substantial, it represents a prudent long-term strategy. By reducing reliance on bottled water and minimizing the risk of waterborne illnesses, these systems offer both financial savings and health benefits over time.

In summary, a home water filtration system not only ensures access to clean and safe drinking water but also serves as a proactive measure to mitigate the risks associated with industrial pollution and other contaminants."

ME to ChatGPT:

Can we make this blog more meaningful to homeowners

ChatGPT

Certainly! Let's tailor the content to resonate more deeply with homeowners:

Title: Safeguarding Your Home and Health: The Power of Home Water Filtration Systems

Introduction: As homeowners, ensuring the safety and well-being of our families is our top priority. Yet, amidst growing concerns about water quality, it's easy to feel uncertain about the water flowing from our taps. Fortunately, there's a simple yet powerful solution: investing in a home water filtration system.

- *Protecting Your Loved Ones:* Think of your home water filter as a silent guardian, tirelessly working to rid your water of harmful contaminants. From industrial pollutants to microbial threats, these systems act as a first line of defense, shielding your loved ones from potential health risks associated with contaminated water.
- *Embracing Peace of Mind:* Imagine the reassurance of knowing that every sip of water you and your family take is clean and safe. With a home filtration system in place, you can enjoy peace of mind, free from the worry of hidden pollutants lurking in your water supply.
- *Preserving Your Home's Sanctuary:* Our homes are more than just buildings; they're sanctuaries where we seek comfort and refuge. By investing in a water filtration system, you're not just protecting your health but also safeguarding the sanctity of your home, ensuring that every drop of water contributes to a healthier, happier living environment.
- *Sustainable Living, One Drop at a Time:* In today's world, sustainability is more than just a buzzword – it's a responsibility we owe to future generations. By reducing reliance on bottled water and minimizing our environmental footprint, home water filtration systems empower homeowners to embrace sustainable living practices, one drop at a time.

 **ChatGPT**

- *Making Informed Choices for Your Home:* As homeowners, we have the power to make informed choices that prioritize the health and well-being of our families. By investing in a home water filtration system, you're not just enhancing your quality of life – you're taking a proactive step towards creating a safer, healthier home for generations to come.

Conclusion: In a world where uncertainty looms large, our homes remain steadfast pillars of safety and security. By embracing the power of home water filtration systems, we're not just safeguarding our health – we're nurturing the very essence of what makes our houses feel like home. So, let's raise a glass – to cleaner, safer, and happier homes for all. Cheers!

This approach aims to connect with homeowners on a personal level, emphasizing the significance of water filtration systems in protecting their homes, families, and peace of mind.

You can see that I asked my AI to change this particular blog 4 times. Remember, your AI does not care if you change this a dozen times until you feel you are both on the same page. You can use pieces of what AI provided. You might decide to ask your AI to re-write this again to make it shorter. You might decide to focus on a particular thread within what your AI wrote.

For example, in the original copy, my AI had a paragraph on sustainable living. Let's see what happens when we refocus the blog on that.

ME to ChatGPT:

Can you refocus this to emphasize sustainable living

ChatGPT

Absolutely! Let's highlight the sustainability aspect of home water filtration systems:

Title: Sustainable Living Starts at Home: The Eco-Friendly Benefits of Water Filtration Systems

Introduction: As stewards of our planet, we're increasingly mindful of the environmental impact of our daily choices. From reducing waste to conserving energy, every decision we make at home plays a part in shaping a more sustainable future. One often-overlooked yet significant step towards eco-friendly living? Investing in a home water filtration system.

- *A Greener Alternative:* Say goodbye to plastic waste! With a home water filtration system, you can significantly reduce your reliance on single-use plastic bottles. By opting for filtered tap water, you're not just saving money – you're also minimizing plastic pollution and taking a stand for a cleaner, greener planet.
- *Preserving Precious Resources:* Water is our most precious resource, yet millions of gallons are wasted each year in the production and transportation of bottled water. By choosing a home filtration system, you're conserving water and energy, making a positive impact on our environment and helping to preserve precious resources for future generations.
- *Sustainable Solutions for Every Home:* Whether you live in a bustling city apartment or a suburban family home, there's a water filtration solution tailored to your needs. From countertop filters to under-the-sink systems, these eco-friendly options offer convenience without compromising on sustainability, proving that sustainable living is within reach for every homeowner.
- *Empowering Eco-Conscious Choices:* As consumers, we have the power to shape the market and drive demand for sustainable alternatives. By choosing a home water filtration system, you're sending a clear message to manufacturers and policymakers that sustainability matters. Together, we can create a world where eco-friendly choices are the norm, not the exception.

ChatGPT

- *Building a Sustainable Legacy:* Our homes are more than just buildings – they're reflections of our values and aspirations for the future. By embracing sustainable solutions like home water filtration systems, we're not just making a difference today – we're building a legacy of environmental stewardship that will endure for generations to come.

Conclusion: In a world where every drop counts, our homes serve as laboratories for sustainable living. By investing in a home water filtration system, we're not just filtering water – we're filtering out waste, pollution, and unsustainable practices, one glass at a time. So let's raise a toast – to a more sustainable future, where every choice we make at home leaves a lasting, positive impact on our planet. Cheers to sustainable living!

This approach emphasizes the role of home water filtration systems in promoting sustainable living practices and encourages homeowners to make eco-friendly choices that benefit both their families and the planet.

What you can see is how AI can modify the wording to stress what you want to feature in your blog. I'm not crazy about the raise a glass /cheers thing – I could ask AI to revise the copy again and omit it.....but I think you get the idea.

ELEVATING SOCIAL MEDIA ENGAGEMENT THROUGH AI

The gal that handled my social media quit the other day. That meant that until I find a replacement, I'm our new social media maven.

So, I had to take a quick course in creating posts – which BTW, is way different than writing blogs and articles. (I am typically a long-form kind of gal)

I also had to learn to enhance the blogs with images/other media.

My ChatGPT has been a wonderful partner to help me fulfill my social medial goals. If I can learn how to do it, so can you!

Using AI to create posts for social media is actually fun. You just need to ask it nicely and give it some parameters. Here's some examples.

ME to ChatGPT:

I need a series of Facebook Posts to promote water quality. Brand name is Dataman Group. location is Boca Raton, Florida. Looking for about 100 words.

ChatGPT

Here's a series of Facebook posts for "Dataman Group" in Boca Raton, Florida, to promote water quality awareness:

Post 1:

" 💧 Let's make every drop count, Boca Raton! At Dataman Group, we believe in protecting our precious water resources. Join us in making a difference. Start with simple steps like fixing leaks and reducing water waste. Together, we can preserve water quality for generations to come! #WaterConservation #BocaRaton"

Post 2:

" 🚰 Tap into cleaner water! Dataman Group is dedicated to educating our community about water quality. Did you know that reducing pollutants starts at home? Avoid using harmful chemicals and opt for eco-friendly products. Let's keep Boca's water safe and clean! #CleanWater #EcoFriendly"

ChatGPT

🌀 **Post 3:**

"   Dive into action with Dataman Group! Protecting Boca Raton's water isn't just about us—it affects all marine life. Support local cleanups and get involved in community efforts to keep our waterways pristine. Every action counts! #MarineConservation #BocaRaton"

👥👥👥 **Post 4:**

"👥👥👥 Community Call! Join Dataman Group in Boca Raton as we host a seminar on water quality this weekend. Learn about your water, how it's treated, and what we can do to ensure it stays clean. Let's educate and empower our community together! #WaterQualityEducation #CommunityEngagement"

These posts blend calls to action with educational content, engaging the local community to participate in preserving water quality.

Love it. That was easy-peasy. But we also know that posts attract more visibility when they are accompanied by a compelling photo.

ME to ChatGPT:
Can you create a post that works with this photo?

ChatGPT

Here's a suggested Facebook post to accompany the photo of a woman drinking water:

Stay Hydrated, Stay Healthy! 💧

Nothing refreshes like a glass of clean, crisp water! At Dataman Group in Boca Raton, we're committed to ensuring everyone has access to safe drinking water. Remember, keeping hydrated is key to maintaining your health. Drink up and enjoy the purity in every sip! 🌊 #CleanWater #HealthFirst #BocaRaton

This post leverages the image to emphasize the importance of water quality and hydration, aligning with your organization's focus on water issues. Notice that AI includes hashtags in their recommended posts.

A NOTE ABOUT HASHTAGS

Hashtags actually serve a purpose in social media by helping people to connect to other people with shared interests.

Hashtags make content discoverable to a broader audience beyond just your followers. By including relevant hashtags, your posts can appear in searches or dedicated streams for those specific tags. This increases your visibility.

Relevant. That's the key word. Sometimes social media users search by hashtag. For example, there may be someone scrolling through looking for #CleanWater. The post example AI provided uses that hashtag. If someone was scrolling and looking for that hashtag, your post could up.

The goal here is by using hashtags wisely, users and brands can enhance their social media strategy to reach a wider audience, participate in relevant conversations, and build community around shared interests or events.

STREAMLINING EMAIL CAMPAIGNS WITH AI

Sometimes we just get stuck getting something started. That's where AI comes in. You can ask it to write an email for you.

For example, let's ask ChatGPT to create an email

ME to ChatGPT:

Please create an email out to send to my customers letting them know we have a special sale on salt for the next month

ChatGPT

Here's a sample email, complete with a subject line, to inform your customers about the special sale on salt:

Subject: Special Month-Long Sale on Salt – Don't Miss Out!

Dear [Customer's Name],

We're excited to announce an exclusive offer just for our valued customers like you! Starting today, we're running a special month-long sale on all our salt products. It's the perfect time to stock up and save!

Exclusive Savings! Enjoy incredible discounts on every purchase of our high-quality salt. Whether you're replenishing your kitchen supplies or gearing up for culinary experiments, our sale has you covered.

Why Our Salt? Our salts are sourced to ensure the highest quality and variety. From cooking and seasoning to health and wellness uses, our products meet all your needs.

Act Now! This special offer is available for a limited time only – from now until the end of the month. Visit our store or order online to take advantage of these great prices.

We're looking forward to helping you make the most of this offer. Thank you for your continued support and loyalty.

Warm regards,

[Your Name]
[Your Position]
[Company Name]
[Contact Information]

P.S. Stay tuned for more exclusive deals by following us on our social media pages!

This email template highlights the sale details, encourages quick action, and maintains a friendly and informative tone to enhance customer engagement.

Not bad. But what if I personalized it more by including the city name. AI is not just going to rewrite the exact same email and add in the city name. It's going to provide a completely new option for your consideration.

ME to ChatGPT:

Can you help me word and email to my customers letting them know we have a special sale on salt for the next month. Mention Boca Raton, FL

ChatGPT

Absolutely! Here's a draft email you can use to inform your customers about the special salt sale happening next month, specifically mentioning Boca Raton, FL:

Subject: Exclusive Salt Sale for Our Boca Raton Customers!

Dear [Customer's Name],

Great news from [Your Business Name]! As one of our valued customers in Boca Raton, FL, we're excited to let you know about an exclusive offer coming your way.

🧂 **Special Month-Long Salt Sale!** 🧂 For the entire next month, we're offering fantastic discounts on our entire range of salt products. Whether you need salt for your kitchen, water softening, or any other purpose, now is the perfect time to stock up and save!

- **Why Choose Our Salt?**
- **Top Quality**: Our salts are sourced for their purity and performance.
- **Variety**: Whatever your need, we have the salt to match.
- **Local Focus**: As a Boca Raton business, we're here to serve our community with the best products and offers.

Sale Details:

- **Location**: [Store Address or Online Store Link]
- **Duration**: [Start Date] to [End Date]
- **Offer**: Enjoy up to [XX]% off on all salt products!

ChatGPT

We encourage you to take advantage of this limited-time offer. Visit us in-store or online to enjoy these special savings. And as always, thank you for supporting local business. We look forward to seeing you soon!

Warm regards,

[Your Name]
[Your Position]
[Your Business Name]
[Contact Information]

This email is designed to engage your local customers with a direct and appealing message about the sale, emphasizing the benefits of the offer and your commitment to the Boca Raton community.

Maybe it's where you want to take your email/maybe not, but personalization is key to the customer experience. You want them to feel special. You know their name. You know where they live, you know what they need.

You get the idea of editing – be specific in your prompting. Edit, replace, use your own words. Use your AI to get you started. But always remember, you are the final say.

Now it's time to make sure you have a subject line that compels your users to open and read it.

BOOSTING OPEN RATES: AI-ENHANCED EMAIL SUBJECT LINES

It was very nice of my AI to provide a subject line for the email. But is it the right one? Will it resonate with the readers?

One of the best things about direct marketing (yes, email marketing is part of the direct marketing genre) is the ability to test. In this case, testing subject lines can make a difference in the open rate of your email.

The subject line is the first thing the recipient sees and it can make the difference in whether the email is opened or ignored. Our goal is to boost those open rates.

I asked my AI about the subject line alternatives for this email

ME to ChatGPT:

Please provide several subject line options for this email

ChatGPT

Certainly! Here are several subject line options for your email about the special sale on salt in Boca Raton:

1. Save Big on Salt This Month at [Your Business Name] in Boca Raton!
2. Boca Raton Exclusive: Month-Long Salt Sale at [Your Business Name]!
3. Special Offer for Boca Raton: Discounts on All Salt Products!
4. Don't Miss Out! Salt Sale Spectacular in Boca Raton
5. Boca Raton Customers: Enjoy Exclusive Salt Savings in [Month]!
6. Savor the Savings: Special Salt Sale Just for Boca Raton!
7. Exclusive for Boca Raton: Major Salt Discounts All Month Long!

These subject lines are designed to catch the eye by highlighting the exclusivity of the offer for Boca Raton and emphasizing the significant savings, aiming to drive higher open rates.

When it comes to testing, call my friends over at Lamplight Media. They are the queens of this kind of testing.

THE ART OF AI-GENERATED IMAGERY

I used DALL.E to create some images for some of my material. I am just a beginner with image creation (OK – some of you saw my avatar with the weird moving mouth) but like many of you, I wear lot of hats at my business. And, just like you I am learning more and more about AI and improving my skills.

As I said earlier, prompting is key. And, since I am using AI platforms that I can converse with in regular English, I know that providing as much information as I can will give me the best result.

ME to DALL.E:

Please create an image for a <u>New Homeowner Welcome Campaign</u>: When individuals purchase a new home, it marks a significant milestone in their lives. New Homeowner trigger data is compiled from property records or real estate transactions to identify new homeowners in your target area. I want to show an image that personalizes welcome campaigns tailored specifically to their needs and interests. This could include offering discounts on home décor, handyman services, or home security systems.

DALL.E

Here is an image designed for a New Homeowner Welcome Campaign, capturing the essence of a family's new beginning in their home, complemented by symbols of the services and discounts offered to them.

ME to DALL.E:

Can you revise – let's see another option

DALL.E

Certainly

I've created revised images focusing on a husband, wife, and their two children for the New Homeowner Welcome Campaign.

ME to DALL.E:

Can you please revise the image of the husband, wife and two children - make them a bit smaller so the house is more visible.

DALL.E

Here is a revised image with the family portrayed smaller to emphasize their new home more clearly.

These images are unique and machine-generated. And OK – they are a little scary.

ME to ChatGPT:

Is there a photo on one of the photo sites that is something like this?

ChatGPT

I can't browse the internet, including photo sites, so I'm unable to search for or confirm the availability of specific photos on those platforms. However, you can visit stock photo websites like Shutterstock, Adobe Stock, or Unsplash and use keywords like "new homeowner family", "family in front of house", or "homeowner welcome campaign" to potentially find images that match what you're looking for. These sites often have a wide range of images that could suit your needs.

One more try. I went back to ChatGPT and gave it the same prompt

ME to ChatGPT:

Please create an image for a New Homeowner Welcome Campaign: When individuals purchase a new home, it marks a significant milestone in their lives. New Homeowner trigger data is compiled from property records or real estate transactions to identify new homeowners in your target area. I want to show an image that personalizes welcome campaigns tailored specifically to their needs and interests. This could include offering discounts on home décor, handyman services, or home security systems.

ChatGPT

 **ChatGPT**

Here's an image for your New Homeowner Welcome Campaign that captures a diverse group of new homeowners each holding items symbolizing personalized welcome gifts. This vibrant and welcoming scene is designed to illustrate how your campaign can tailor offerings like home décor, handyman services, or home security systems to new homeowners. Feel free to use this image in your campaign to highlight the personalization of your services.

While these images may be unique and, according to AI, fit my request, I think I'm going to go back to the stock photo sites for more realistic photos.

Like you, I am learning more about AI every day and while I am pretty good using AI for the content part I have a long way to go when it comes to the images.

NAVIGATING AI AND COPYRIGHT LAWS

When I asked my AI to provide me something about marketing to new homeowners (you know I write a lot about that), it actually gave me something I wrote. Personally, I was thrilled that my own work was used to answer my question.

However, many people are not thrilled. As a matter of fact, there are many complaints from artists about AI art generators because they're unhappy about their work being used without their permission. In the visual arts, AI-powered tools can produce content much faster and more affordably than humans, making competition fierce for artists.

In the music industry, more than 200 music artists including stars like Nicki Minaj, Katy Perry, Billie Eilish, Stevie Wonder, J Balvin and Jon Bon Jovi have signed an open letter warning against the "predatory use of AI" in the music industry.

As artificial intelligence (AI) gets better at creating things like art, music, and writing, it brings up some tricky questions about copyright. Normally, copyright laws protect creative works made by humans, but what happens when an AI is doing the creating?

Here's the dilemma: right now, many laws say that only things made by people can be protected by copyright. This means that if an AI creates something on its own, that work might not get any copyright protection because there wasn't a human directly involved in making it.

Also, there's the issue of AI using material that is copyrighted —like training on copyrighted books or songs— to make something new. This can lead to problems if the AI's new creation is too similar to the things it learned from, as it might accidentally copy someone else's protected work.

So, as AI keeps getting more involved in creative fields, we might need to rethink and possibly change our copyright laws to better fit the new technology. It's important for the people making laws, the creators, and those developing AI to talk about these issues and find a good balance that encourages both innovation and respects copyright.

CONCLUSION: THE FUTURE OF AI IN MARKETING

We're just at the beginning. More marketers are using AI than ever before. AI will continue to be more integrated and intuitive and will offer us more options.

For example, in terms of personalization, AI will get even better at understanding individual customer preferences and behaviors. This means marketing can be more tailored to each person, making ads and recommendations feel more relevant and less intrusive. I ca;; this "Marketing to a Universe of One". And, with print on demand, totally possible to do cost-effectively.

More of the routine and repetitive tasks in marketing will be automated by AI. This frees up marketers to focus on creative and strategic tasks that machines can't handle as well.

AI will help marketers be more efficient by analyzing large amounts of data quickly. This means they can see what's working and what isn't in real time, and make smarter decisions without spending weeks on research.

AI will improve how businesses interact with customers, using chatbots and virtual assistants that are becoming increasingly sophisticated. These tools can handle customer questions and problems almost instantly, at any time of the day.

Last, AI's role in content creation will grow, helping to generate written content, visuals, and even videos that are customized for different audiences and platforms. That will allow you to target specific segments more effectively. For example, if your media is being directed at families with children, when you prompt your AI that this is your target audience, the content it creates will be more relevant for this group.

Overall, AI is set to make marketing more effective, less costly, and more exciting by enabling more creative, targeted, and engaging strategies.

Last comment - always remember that AI is not the end-all/be-all. AI does not have your human intuition about your Dealership and the special nuances of your business.

Use AI as your marketing assistant – but always remember that you're the Boss!

ABOUT THE AUTHOR: DALE "DATA DALE" FILHABER

Dale "Data Dale" Filhaber is President & Listologist Supreme of Dataman Group Direct, a Florida-based direct marketing company founded in 1981.

DataDale is a well-known author, lecturer and direct marketing commentator. In the past 35+ years, she has trained many water quality dealers in direct marketing and lead generation techniques, ranging from direct mail to telemarketing to social media.

DataDale has published many articles in Water Conditioning Products and Water Technology magazines & is the author of Pure Water Profits, a blog on marketing for the water quality industry. She is a Water Quality Association member and a frequent guest lecturer at annual WQA conferences.

This new book "Artificial Intelligence in Water Quality Marketing: A Practical Guide to AI-Powered Lead Generation" was inspired by the response to Data Dale's presentations at the 2023 and 2024 WQA conferences. This is Data Dale's sixth book. It is available on Amazon.

"Lead Generation for Water Quality Dealers – 2023 edition'" is also available on Amazon. This book focuses on giving Dealers, marketing directors and sales managers the tools they need to develop an integrated marketing program to boost the number of leads they bring into their dealerships.

First released in 2017, "Lead Generation for Water Quality Dealers" was heralded as a must read for water dealers. Her first book, "Lead Generation Made Easier", has generated over 1,000 downloads.

DataDale can be reached at dale@datamangroup.com

DATAMAN GROUP DIRECT

The team at Dataman Group Direct has been providing lead generation data for Water Quality Dealerships for over 38 years. The company is best known for the Dataman New Homeowner list, which has become the backbone of every Dealer's marketing program.

Dataman Group offers a broad menu of lists geared to generate leads at every Dealership, including New Homeowners, Homeowners with Children, Ailment Sufferers, Health-Conscious Consumers, Eco-Conscious Homeowners, Businesses as well as Homeowners with Modeled Credit.

Dataman Group also helps Dealers analyze their customer lists and append telephone numbers, e-mail addresses and cell phone numbers to their data, creating multifaceted lists for a blended omni-channel marketing experience.

Check out Dataman Group's new postcard portal, myDMpostcards.com. With no minimums, this service is great for weekly new homeowner and monthly maintenance mailings.

Dataman Group Direct is committed to the Water Quality Industry and the Water Quality Research Foundation.

Dealers and marketing managers are invited to visit the section of Dataman Group's dedicated to the water treatment industry.

The Dataman Group Team can be reached at (800) 771-3282

www.ingramcontent.com/pod-product-compliance
Lightning Source LLC
Chambersburg PA
CBHW070141230526
45472CB00004B/1630